TABLE OF CONTENTS

CU00942355

INTRODUCTION

Baking is enjoying somewhat of a revival!

There is something truly wonderful about making something with your own hands, from scratch, using ingredients that you have in your cupboard. It's almost like magic - you create, you cook, and voila! A delicious treat to enjoy with your family, or by yourself if you prefer!

Some people are a little nervous about baking. They assume it's difficult and it requires a lot of knowledge beforehand. The truth is that's not the case. Yes, baking does require a few basic skills, but these can easily be learnt. Techniques aren't difficult to master, and with trial and error you'll find that your baking masterpieces slowly begin to improve in quality.

To help you bypass the trial and error stage and jump straight to baking genius, this book is going to give you all the information you need to start baking delicious cakes, cookies, brownies, breads, the list goes on!

All you need are a few basic ingredients and equipment that you probably already have lurking in your cupboard, such as mixing bowls and baking sheets. There is nothing particularly difficult here, and you don't require all singing, all dancing kitchen equipment to whip up a batch of seriously impressive cookies!

So, if you're ready to learn how to bake up a storm, read our preparation chapters, soak up the knowledge you need, choose your first recipe, and get started!

HOW TO PREPARE YOUR KITCHEN FOR BAKING SUCCESS!

Baking itself isn't hard, as we've already mentioned, but you can have minor baking disasters if you don't do the groundwork beforehand. All you need to do is arrange and prepare your kitchen to make life a little easier.

In this chapter, we'll cover all of that and more.

First things first, tidy up!

Step 1 - Clear Out Your Cupboards

You'll probably have all the basic baking utensils you need in your cupboards, they're simply gathering dust at the back because they're not being used regularly! The best approach? Clear out your cupboards.

Take everything out, decide whether you need it or not, be ruthless if possible, and declutter as best you can. Anything you choose to keep, give it a good clean. If anything is broken, don't be tempted to keep it, throw it out and buy new.

This step also means that you can find out what you have lurking in those cupboards, things you probably forgot you had!

Step 2 - Replace or Purchase The Basics You Need

After you've sorted out your cupboards and looked at what you have versus what you don't have, it's time to go shopping. To create delicious treats you'll need just a few basic equipment pieces, and these will last you for a long time to come, being used over and over again.

You will need:
- Mixing bowls, small, medium, and large
- Spatula
- Wooden spoon
- Sieve
- Cake tins
- Baking trays
- Parchment paper
- Pastry brush
- Metal tongs
- Whisk
- Cooling rack
- Weighing scales
- Teaspoon and tablespoon
- Measuring cups
- Measuring jug

That's it. These are also items you can use in everyday cooking, so you're not splashing the cash for no good reason. There is one other decision you need to make - should you purchase a stand mixer?

It's a personal choice. It's a good piece of equipment to have and these don't always cost a huge amount of cash. They're also very versatile and you'll find yourself using them many times for many different reasons.

A stand mixer with various attachments means that your baking will come together far easier and far quicker. The quality is also likely to be higher because you can be sure that ingredients are combined properly - flour in particular can be very difficult to completely combine without using an electric mixer.

If you choose to purchase a mixer, shop around and find the best deal. You don't need an all singing, all dancing food processor if you're simply going to start with baking. A stand mixer with standard attachments is enough. If you can find one with a bread hook attachment, that's a good buy too.

Step 3 - Arrange Your Cupboards

Once you have all your equipment, it's time to arrange your cupboards in a clean and tidy way, so everything is organised and easy to find. It's a good idea to invest in some plastic storage boxes here, so you can keep things arranged with ease, and not have all your utensils falling all over the place and being lost.

You can take this opportunity to give your cupboards a really good clean out too - it's very satisfying!

Step 4 - Keep Your Stock of Basic Baking Ingredients Updated

You don't have to go out and buy everything single baking ingredient, because you're going to start with one recipe and go from there, however there are some store cupboard basics that are useful to have, should the baking bug bite you at a random time of the day.

If you decide to bake a treat that requires something you don't have, you can simply put it on your shopping list and make it the next time you go shopping, but the basics you should have in your cupboards and refrigerator at all times are:

- Flour - plain and self-raising flour
- Eggs
- Milk
- Caster sugar
- Icing sugar
- Brown sugar
- Butter
- Jam
- Baking powder
- Bicarbonate soda
- Vanilla essence or powder

These basics will allow you to whip up a basic cake or batch of cookies if you have a sweet craving at a random time of the day, or even the night!

Step 5 - Purchase Storage Boxes

We already mentioned plastic storage boxes to arrange your cupboards, but what about when you've baked something and you want it to last for a few days?

A series of plastic storage boxes means you can keep everything fresh, either in the fridge or at room temperature, without worrying about anything flying in or your cookies going soft. These are really useful things to have in general life anyway, so they're certainly not going to be a fad investment.

Step 6 - Get Baking!

You now have everything in place to get started and you have a perfectly arranged kitchen to have success too! Make sure you identify a specific part of the kitchen where you'll do all your weighing out of ingredients and mixing etc, usually a larger part of your kitchen counter so that you can clean it down easily after you've finished.

There's no need to start with the basics and work up, recipes are very easy to follow and you can begin with whatever you want, taking your time and working through the instructions. If you get stuck with techniques etc, just head onto YouTube and watch a video demonstration!

Baking is a fantastic activity. You can do it with your children, you can do it when you're alone, you can do it simply because you want a little chill out time, and the end result is something delicious to enjoy.

What's not to like?

WHAT DO I NEED TO KNOW BEFORE I START?

There's not a whole lot you need to know beforehand but there are some tips and tricks you can use throughout your baking adventure, to give you better results.

Baking is an art form, but it's one that's enjoyable as you learn. Let's be honest, even a cake that sinks centrally still tastes amazing, so there are no failures to be had when cooking delicious treats!

Always remember to double check the dates on your baking ingredients. Baking powder in particular needs to be well in date before you use it. This is because it loses its power over time and it won't activate when baking to give your cake/whatever you're baking enough rise.

It's also a good idea to buy quality ingredients, rather than cheap and cheerful. Yes, flour is flour, but there are certain ingredients which work better when they're a higher quality. Baking powder is one of them, but any baking spices you need to use should be fresh and the best quality you can get your hands on, if possible. This simply gives your baking the edge and helps it to taste as delicious as possible.

Let's look at a few useful tips and techniques you can incorporate into your baking routine, to ensure the best outcomes.

Tips & Techniques

Tip 1 - Take The Time to Prepare

Before you dive in and start creating something delicious, it's important that you read the recipe through and ensure you have all the ingredients and enough of them. Then, you should measure out your ingredients so that you have them to hand.

Many people make the mistake of measuring as they go along but this is not only a stressful approach but it means that the mixture or batter is left standing for too long as you're measuring out the next ingredient to add. This isn't a huge problem with all recipes, but in some cases it can mean the outcome won't be as good.

You'll enjoy baking far more if you're organised, so do a little preparation beforehand and understand the recipe you're going to attempt.

Tip 2 - Understand Measuring And Weighing

For your baking to be a success, you have to ensure measuring and weighing of ingredients is spot on. Let's give an example - if you are following a recipe that asks for 2 cups of flour, you have to identify where the cut off point on the cup is, and level the flour out on top, therefore ensuring you don't use too much flour. If you do this, in a cake especially, the batter won't cook properly and the cake will be heavy.

Recipes are created with measurements for a good reason - the recipe needs those particular measurements in order to work! Simply throwing ingredients in and using guesswork is very unlikely to bring you the results you want.

Dry ingredients, such as sugar and flour will be measured in grams or ounces, but you can also measure them in spoons or cups. Again, make sure you fill it up then use a knife to level the top.

When you're measuring wet ingredients, such as flour, water, etc, you will use millilitres or cups. You can use a measuring jug for this or you can use a cup with millilitres on the side. Go with whatever works for you, but make sure that you get the measurement spot on, to avoid the mixture becoming too wet and therefore not baking properly in the oven.

When you're using your weighing scales, make sure that you get the number as close to the desired amount as possible, and spot on if you possibly can.

Tip 3 - Be Cautious When Using Butter

When a recipe calls for butter, you might be tempted to just throw a lump into the mixer and let the machine do the work. The problem is, the butter needs to be the right consistency for the particular recipe you're following, otherwise the end result won't be as good as you want it to be.

Check the recipe and follow the instructions. The common instructions you'll see are softened, melted and chilled.

Of course, everyone has a different idea of what softened actually means! Basically, when a recipe asks for softened butter, it means it's at room temperature and it's easy to stir and mix. It shouldn't be wet or warm per se, but it should be easily malleable. Leaving your butter out of the fridge for around an hour should be enough but if it's a particular hot day, perhaps half an hour should be sufficient.

When a recipe asks for chilled butter it means it's a lot firmer, but not solid. When you use a knife on the butter, it flakes and it's quite hard to cut. In most recipes that ask for chilled butter, you'll be asked to cut it into cubes and rub it into the flour using your hands, particularly when you're making crumbles or pastry for pies.

That leaves us with melted butter. Pretty simple, right? Yes, but it shouldn't be hot. After you've melted the butter, you need to let it cool a little so that it's still a little warm but you can easily stand it when you put your finger inside. If you use melted butter that's too hot and pour it into your mixing bowl, it's basically going to cook the ingredients a little - you really don't want scrambled eggs in the middle of a cake!

Tip 4 - Know What Room Temperature Really Means

You'll see some recipes asking for 'room temperature' ingredients, such as eggs or butter. So, what exactly counts as room temperature?

Basically, as long as your room isn't extremely hot or cold, you've got a suitable temperature for your ingredients. Take them out of the fridge and leave them for around an hour, to be level with the temperature in the room. When they reach that point, you can use them in the recipe, knowing that they're going to have the desired effect.

Tip 5 - Do Not Open The Oven Door!

You're going to be excited and you'll want to check that your cake is rising or that your pie is golden. That's understandable, but if you keep opening the door to the oven you're going to throw off the temperature and it's going to affect how well the item bakes.

When you allow cooler air to make its way inside the oven, it has the effect of deflating anything that's cooking. The heat is causing a reaction within the ingredients, to get them to rise. When you're interfering and letting in cold air, the result won't be what you want. Be patient!

For this reason, make sure that you set your oven timer properly and rely upon that to tell you when the item should be cooked.

Tip 6 - Check That Your Baking is Finished

We just mentioned relying upon your oven timer, but sometimes when the timer goes off, the item you're baking still needs another few minutes. The most effective way is to use toothpick and insert it into the centre of whatever you're cooking. With a cake recipe, if the toothpick is totally clean, it's cooked. If you see any remnants of the batter on the toothpick, it needs a little longer.

However, when doing this, don't leave the oven door open too long - test quickly and close th door once more.

Tip 7 - Use Parchment or Foil to Stop The Tops of Cakes Burning

Sometimes, no matter how well you set your oven, the top of a cake can cook far faster than the bottom, leaving you with a burnt top section and a rather uncooked middle or bottom section. This is a common problem, but you can overcome it by carefully laying a measured sheet of baking parchment or foil on top when you notice it starting to burn. This protects the top section and gives the rest enough time to catch up.

These few tips should help you to achieve baking success far quicker than if you had no knowledge at all. All that's left to do now is for you to choose the first recipe you want to try, and see how you get on!

RECIPES

RECIPES

CAKES

TRADITIONAL VICTORIA SANDWICH

Time 30 minutes, serves 10

Net carbs: 76g/2.6oz, Fiber: 0.6g/0.02oz, Fat: 28g/0.98oz,

Protein: 5g/0.17oz, Kcal: 558

INGREDIENTS:

- ◆ 200g/7oz regular sugar
- ◆ 200g/7oz butter, softened to room temperature
- ◆ 4 medium beaten eggs
- ◆ 200g/oz self-raising flour
- ◆ 2 tbsp semi-skimmed milk
- ◆ 1 teaspoon of baking powder
- ◆ 100g/3.5oz softened butter for the filling
- ◆ 140g/5oz sifted icing sugar
- ◆ 170g/6oz strawberry jam (or your preferred flavour)

PREPARATION:

1. Take two 20cm sized sandwich tins and grease or line with baking paper
2. Take a large bowl and combine the caster sugar, 200g/7oz of butter, beaten eggs, flour, milk, baking powder, into a smooth consistency
3. Pour the batter equally between the tins
4. Heat your oven to 190C/374F, or gas mark 5
5. Bake for 20 minutes. The cakes are done when the top s golden brown and the top springs back up when touched
6. Turn the sandwich tins onto a rack and allow to cool
7. Meanwhile, combine the icing sugar and butter until smooth
8. Once the cakes are completely cooled, spread the butter/sugar filling onto one cake
9. Add the jam as another layer
10. Place the remaining sponge on top and sprinkle with icing sugar for decoration.

CARROT CAKE

Time 60 minutes, serves 15
Net carbs: 39g/1.37oz, Fiber: 1g/0.03oz, Fat: 12g/0.42oz,
Protein: 3g/0.10oz, Kcal: 265

INGREDIENTS:

- 175ml cooking oil, either sunflower or olive oil
- 175g/6oz brown sugar
- 3 beaten eggs
- 100g/3.5oz raisins
- 140g/5oz carrot, skins removed and grated
- 175g/6oz of self-raising flour
- Zest of a large orange
- 1 tsp of cinnamon, ground
- 1 tsp bicarbonate soda
- 0.5 tsp freshly grated nutmeg
- 175g/6oz icing sugar
- 2 tbsp orange juice

PREPARATION:

1. Take an 18cm cake tin (square) and line with baking paper
2. Take a large mixing bowl and combine the brown sugar, eggs and oil
3. Add the carrots, raisins, and zest and mix
4. Sift flour, soda, nutmeg and cinnamon and combine again until smooth but slightly loose
5. Pour the mixture into the cake tin
6. Heat the oven to 180C/356F, or gas mark 4
7. Cook the cake for around 45 minutes. The cake is firm yet springs back when you press the middle
8. Turn the cake out onto a cooling rack and cool
9. Meanwhile, combine the orange juice and icing sugar until you achieve a smooth consistency
10. Once cool, place the cake on a plate and drizzle the sugar mixture on top, in zig zag lines.

CLASSIC LEMON DRIZZLE CAKE

Time 60 minutes, serves 10

Net carbs: 50g/1.76oz, Fiber: 1g/0.03oz, Fat: 21g/0.74oz,

Protein: 5g/0.17oz, Kcal: 399

INGREDIENTS:

- ◆ 4 medium eggs
- ◆ 225g/8oz softened butter
- ◆ 225g/8oz self-raising flour
- ◆ 225g/8oz caster sugar
- ◆ Zest of 1 lemon
- ◆ Juice of 1.5 lemons
- ◆ Additional 85g/3oz caster sugar for the topping

PREPARATION:

1. Take a medium bowl and add the sugar and softened butter
2. Beat with a stand mixer or wooden spoon, creating a pale consistency, without any lumps
3. One at a time, add the eggs and combine
4. Use a sieve to sift in the flour and combine carefully
5. Add the zest and combine once more
6. Preheat oven to 180C/356F, or gas mark 4
7. Line a loaf tin, approximately 8x21cm in size with parchment
8. Add the mixture into the loaf tin and level the top
9. Bake for around 45 minutes, until the centre is cooked
10. Allow to cool in the tin
11. In a small mixing bowl, combine the juice with the rest of the caster sugar, to create a drizzle
12. Prick holes in the top of the cake using a fork
13. Pour the drizzle mixture over the cake allowing it to run into the sponge
14. Place the cake aside to cool. Remove from the tin and slice into pieces

WALNUT & COFFEE CAKE

Time 75 minutes, serves 10

Net carbs: 55g/1.94oz, Fiber: 2g/0.07oz, Fat: 41g/1.44oz,

Protein: 7g/0.24oz, Kcal: 620

INGREDIENTS:

- ◆ 250g/9oz softened butter
- ◆ 280g/10oz self-raising flour
- ◆ 250g/9oz caster sugar
- ◆ 4 medium eggs
- ◆ 100ml strong coffee (black, and made with 2 tbsp granules)
- ◆ 1 tsp vanilla extract
- ◆ 0.5 tsp vanilla extract
- ◆ 2 tbsp roughly chopped walnuts
- ◆ 4 tbsp finely chopped walnuts
- ◆ 100g/3.5oz icing sugar
- ◆ 150ml cream (double cream works best)
- ◆ 100g/3.5oz mascarpone (you can use good quality cream cheese if you can't find mascarpone)

PREPARATION:

1. Take a large bowl and mix together the sugar, baking powder, butter, and vanilla

2. Add the coffee to the bowl, keeping 1 tbsp to one side

3. Use a whisk or mixer to create a smooth and creamy consistency

4. Add the walnuts (finely chopped), and fold them into the batter with a spatula, distributing evenly

5. Preheat your oven to 180C/356F, or gas mark 4

6. Take two round cake tins, approximately 2 x 20cm sized, and prepare with baking parchment

7. Pour the batter into the cake tins, making sure you have even amounts

8. Add the remaining walnuts (roughly chopped) over the top of one of the cakes, scattering evenly

9. Place the cakes into the oven and bake for around 30 minutes

10. Take the cake without the walnuts on top and add the remaining 1 tbsp of coffee over the top

11. Place both cakes to one side, cooling in the tins

12. As the cakes are cooling, take a medium mixing bowl and combine the mascarpone, cream and the icing sugar until smooth

13. Once the cakes are cooled, spread the mixture over both sides of cake and sandwich together

14. Ice the top of the cake and add the remaining walnuts for decoration

DECADENT CHOCOLATE CAKE

Time 55 minutes, serves 12-14
Net carbs: 59g/2oz, Fiber: 2g/0.07oz, Fat: 29g/1.02oz,
Protein: 6g/0.21oz, Kcal: 523

INGREDIENTS:

- 200g/7oz softened butter
- 200g/7oz caster sugar
- 4 medium eggs
- 2 tbsp good quality cocoa powder
- 200g/7oz self-raising flour
- 1 tsp baking powder
- 2 tbsp milk
- 0.5 tsp vanilla extract
- 100g/3.5oz chopped milk chocolate
- 200g/7oz softened butter for the filling
- 5 tbsp/oz cocoa powder for the filling
- 400g/14oz icing sugar
- 2 tbsp milk for the filling

PREPARATION:

1. In a large mixing bowl, combine the sugar, butter, eggs, baking powder, flour, cocoa powder, milk and vanilla to create a smooth batter

2. Preheat your oven to 190C/374F, or gas mark 5

3. Take two round cake tins, 20cm in size, and prepare them with baking parchment

4. Pour the the batter evenly into each cake tin

5. Bake for around 20 minutes

6. Cool for 15 minutes and turn turn them out of the tins onto a cooling rack

7. Meanwhile, take a heatproof bowl and add the chocolate

8. Place the bowl into the microwave and melt, giving it a quick stir every 30 minutes

9. Once melted, place to one side for a few minutes

10. Take another bowl and pour in the butter and icing sugar

11. Combine together using a fork to create a mixture and then use an electric mixer to create a smoother consistency

12. Use a sieve to add the cocoa powder and combine

13. Pour the melted chocolate into the mixture and the milk, mixing until completely combined

14. Once the cakes are cooled, spread half of the filling on one side of the cake. Repeat with the other side

15. Sandwich the cakes together and sprinkle a little icing sugar over the top

DECADENT CHOCOLATE CAKE

APRICOT FRUIT CAKE

Time 85 minutes, serves 12

Net carbs:56g/1.97oz, Fiber: 3g/0.1oz, Fat: 27g/0.95oz,

Protein: 7g/0.24oz, Kcal: 486

INGREDIENTS:

- 4 tbsp good quality sherry (optional)
- 140g/5oz sultanas
- 140g5/oz chopped dried apricots
- 50g/1.7oz flaked almonds
- 100g/3.5oz ground almonds
- 140g/5oz chopped dried apricots
- 140g/5oz mixed peel
- 250g/9oz softened butter
- 1 tsp baking powder
- 250g/9oz brown sugar
- 1 tsp vanilla extract
- 200g/7oz plain flour
- 3 beaten eggs
- Zest and juice of 1 orange
- Juice and zest of 1 lemon

PREPARATION:

1. Place the sultanas and sherry in a bowl and leave to soak for around 60 minutes - omit this step if you are not using sherry

2. Take a medium mixing bowl and combine the sugar, vanilla, butter until pale

3. Add one egg at a time and mix until a smooth consistency forms

4. Add the baking powder and flour stir in gently to combine

5. Add the flaked and ground almonds and combine

6. Add the soaked sultanas and any remaining sherry left over and combine

7. Add the mixed peel, zest, juice, and the dried apricots and combine everything tougher well

8. Preheat the oven to 160C/320F, or gas mark 3

9. Take a spring bottomed cake tin. Size 23cm is enough but make sure it is also quite deep, and line it with parchment, up the sides

10. Transfer the cake into the tin and make sure the top is smooth

11. Bake for 1 hour and 20 minutes. It is done when a toothpick is clean

12. Keep the cake in the tin to cool before turning out and storing for no more than one month in a storage box

STICKY CARAMEL CAKE

Time 60 minutes, serves 12-14

Net carbs: 62g/2oz, Fiber: 1g/0.03oz, Fat: 28g/1oz,

Protein: 5g/0.17oz, Kcal: 517

INGREDIENTS:

- ♦ 125g/4.5oz caster sugar
- ♦ 225g/8oz softened butter
- ♦ 1 tsp vanilla extract
- ♦ 4 medium eggs
- ♦ 100g/3.5oz brown sugar
- ♦ 225g/8oz self-raising flour
- ♦ 2 tbsp milk
- ♦ 200g/7oz softened butter for the filling
- ♦ 400g/14oz icing sugar
- ♦ 70g/2.5oz caramel sauce, and extra for topping

PREPARATION:

1. Take a medium bowl and add the caster sugar, butter, and brown sugar

2. Beat with a wooden spoon or electric mixer until they are smooth

3. Add the eggs individually and beat once more

4. Add the vanilla and combine again

5. Add the milk and flour and combine until smooth

6. Preheat your oven to 180C/F, or gas mark 4

7. Take two springform baking tins, 20cm in size and prepare with baking parchment

8. Distribute the mixture between the two baking tins and even out the top

9. Bake for half an hour

10. Let the cake cool for a short while and then turn onto a cooling rack

11. Meanwhile, take a medium mixing bowl and add the icing sugar and butter

12. Use an electric mixer to combine into a smooth consistency

13. Add the caramel sauce and combine. If you need to loosen the icing mixture, add a little boiling water, but no more than 1 tbsp

14. Once the sponges are cooled, spread the icing on both sides and sandwich the cakes together

15. Spread the rest of the icing on top and smooth the edges down

16. Drizzle a little caramel sauce over the top and decorate with toffee piece if you like

WHITE CHOCOLATE & CITRUS CAKE

Time 70 minutes, serves 10
Net carbs: 45g/1.58oz, Fiber: 1g/0.03oz, Fat: 40g/1.4oz,
Protein: 9g/0.32oz, Kcal: 567

INGREDIENTS:

- ♦ 175g/6oz caster sugar
- ♦ 175g/6oz softened butter
- ♦ 4 medium eggs, with yolks and whites separated into different bowls
- ♦ Zest of 4 oranges
- ♦ Juice of 1 orange
- ♦ 100g/3.5oz self-raising flour
- ♦ 100g/3.5oz ground almonds
- ♦ 1 tsp baking powder
- ♦ 200g/7oz white chocolate
- ♦ 200ml creme fraiche

PREPARATION:

1. Take a medium mixing bowl and add the sugar, butter, and the zest. Combine together with an electric mixer for 60 seconds, until pale

2. Pour in the yolks and combine once more

3. Use a sieve to add the flour and baking powder, folding into the mixture carefully

4. Add the juice and almonds and combine

5. Take a separate bowl and add the egg whites, whisking until just firm

6. Take a third of the egg whites and fold them into the cake mixture

7. Add the other two thirds in sections and combine carefully

8. Preheat your oven to 180C/356F, or gas mark 4

9. Take tow round cake tins, 20cm in size, and prepare with parchment paper

10. Pour the cake mixture evenly between the two cake tins

11. Bake in the oven for 30 minutes, or until cooked

12. Cool for a few minutes and then turn out onto a cooling rack

13. Meanwhile, take a small pan and melt the white chocolate over a low heat

14. Add the creme fraiche into a mixing bowl and whip using an electric mixer, until it thickens

15. Add the white chocolate once cooled and combine once more

16. Once the cakes are cooled, spread the icing onto both cakes and sandwich together

17. Add the rest of the icing on top of the cake and smooth over

18. Refrigerate for an hour before serving

DELICIOUS SYRUP SPONGE

Time 50 minutes, serves 8
Net carbs: 70g/2.5oz, Fiber: 0.9g/0.03oz, Fat: 23g/0.81oz,
Protein: 5.6g/1oz, Kcal: 512

INGREDIENTS:

- 200g/7oz softened butter
- 3 large eggs
- 200g/7oz self-raising flour
- 250g/8.8oz golden syrup/treacle
- Zest of 1 lemon
- Juice of half a lemon
- 5 tbsp breadcrumbs
- 5 tbsp milk

PREPARATION:

1. Take a large mixing bowl and add the zest, breadcrumbs, juice and golden syrup/treacle. Combine together well

2. Take a medium baking dish, around 1.5 litres in size and add the combined mixture at the bottom, pressing down gently

3. Take a mixing bowl and combine the eggs and sugar to form a pale and smooth consistency

4. Beat the eggs into the mixture, one by one

5. Add the milk and flour and stir in by hand until combined

6. Spread the mixture over the top of the baking dish

7. Preheat your oven to 180C/356F, or gas mark 4

8. Bake for 40 minutes

9. Serve with ice cream or custard once slightly cooled

CLASSIC RASPBERRY BAKEWELL

Time 60 minutes, serves 8

Net carbs: 35g/1.2oz, Fiber: 3g/0.1oz, Fat: 28g/0.98oz,

Protein: 8g/0.28oz, Kcal: 411

INGREDIENTS:

- 140g/5oz softened butter
- 140g/5oz ground almonds
- 140g/5oz caster sugar
- 2 medium eggs
- 140g/5oz self-raising flour
- 1 tsp vanilla extract

- 2 tbsp flaked almonds
- 250g/9oz raspberries, fresh or frozen (defrost before use)
- A little icing sugar for dusting the cake

PREPARATION:

1. Use a food processor or blender or to mix the almonds, flour, eggs, vanilla extract, sugar, and butter

2. Preheat the oven to 180C/356F, or gas mark 4

3. Take a springform cake tin, 20cm in size, and prepare with baking parchment

4. Poor half the mixture into the cake tin, making sure the top is smooth

5. Add the raspberries on top

6. Add the the rest of the cake mixture on top and smooth once more

7. Bake for around 50 minutes

8. Once cooled, turn the cake out and add a little icing sugar for decoration

UPSIDE DOWN PINEAPPLE CAKE

Time 55 minutes, serves 6

Net carbs: 49g/1.7oz, Fiber: 1g/0.03oz, Fat: 23g/0.8oz,

Protein: 5g/0.17oz, Kcal: 407

INGREDIENTS:

- 100g/3.5oz softened butter
- 100g/3.5oz caster sugar
- 100g/3.5oz self-raising flour
- 1 tsp vanilla extract
- 1 tsp baking powder
- 2 medium eggs
- 50g/1.7oz brown sugar for the topping
- 50g/1.7oz softened butter for the topping
- 7 glace cherries
- 7 pineapple rings, including the tinned syrup

PREPARATION:

1. In a medium mixing bowl, add 50g/oz of the softened butter and 50g/oz brown sugar, mixing together until as smooth as possible

2. Take a round baking tin, 20cm in size, and add the mixture into the bottom, allowing the mixture to go a little up the sides of the tin

3. Take the pineapple rings and arrange them over the mixture

4. Add the glace cherries in the middle of the pineapple rings

5. In a mixing bowl, add the remaining butter, sugar, flour, baking powder, eggs, and vanilla extract and combine together well

6. Add the syrup from the pineapples and combine once more to create a smooth and soft consistency

7. Add the mixture over the top of the pineapples and smooth over

8. Preheat the oven to 180C/356F, or gas mark 4

9. Bake for around 35 minutes

10. Cool for 5 minutes and then turn the cake onto a serving plate

11. Serve with ice cream whilst just warm

TROPICAL COCONUT CAKE

Time 75 minutes, serves 10

Net carbs: 96g/3.4oz, Fiber: 4g/0.14oz, Fat: 37g/1.3oz,

Protein: 11g/0.38oz, Kcal: 731

INGREDIENTS:

- 3 tbsp groundnut oil
- 5 medium eggs
- 200g/7oz chopped, creamed coconut
- 2 tsp vanilla extract
- 200g/7oz soft cheese
- 600g/21oz caster sugar
- 175g/6oz desiccated coconut
- 375g/13oz plain four
- A little icing sugar for dusting

PREPARATION:

1. Place the creamed coconut into a saucepan allow it to melt using a low heat

2. Add the groundnut oil and combine

3. Remove from heat and pour into a small mixing bowl to cool

4. Take a medium mixing bowl and add the soft cheese and sugar, combine well and add to the coconut oil mixture, stirring well

5. Add the eggs individually and combine

6. Add the vanilla. Combine everything once more

7. Once the mixture has become like a mousse, fold in the flour and coconut until everything is combined and fluffy

8. Preheat your oven to 160C/320F, or gas mark 3

9. Take a deep baking tin, around 20x30cm in size, and prepare with baking parchment

10. Add the mixture to the tin and bake for 60 minutes, or until cooked

11. Turn the cake out onto a cooling rack

12. Dust with a little icing sugar to serve

TANGY HONEY CAKE

Time 90 minutes, serves 12

Net carbs: 43g/1.5oz, Fiber: 1g/0.03oz, Fat: 17g/0.6oz,

Protein: 4g/0.14oz, Kcal: 336

INGREDIENTS:

- 250g/9oz honey, and a little extra for the topping
- 100g/3.5oz dark brown sugar
- 225g/7.9oz chilled butter
- 300g/10.5oz self-raising flour
- 3 beaten eggs

PREPARATION:

1. Heat a small pan over a medium heat
2. Cube the butter and place in the pan. Add the honey and sugar, stirring until melted
3. Bring to the boil for 60 seconds
4. Take the pan from the heat and allow to cool for 20 minutes
5. In a medium mixing bowl, use a wooden spoon to beat the eggs
6. Use a sieve to add the flour to a separate mixing bowl
7. Add the eggs and the cooled honey, and stir until everything is combined
8. Preheat your oven to 140C/284F or gas mark 3
9. Take a springform cake tin, 20cm in size, and prepare with baking parchment
10. Pour the mixture into your baking tin and bake for 1 hour
11. Turn the cake out onto a cooling rack
12. Pour a little honey (around 2 tbsp) to a small saucepan and warm up
13. Brush the honey over the top of the cake sparingly and allow to cool

CHOCOLATE & BEETROOT CAKE

Time 75 minutes, serves 8

Net carbs: 71g/2.5oz, Fiber: 3g/0.10oz, Fat: 34g/1.19oz,

Protein: 7g/0.24oz, Kcal: 594

INGREDIENTS:

- 200g/7oz plain flour
- 100g/3.5oz cocoa powder
- 250g/9oz caster sugar
- 3 medium eggs
- 2 tsp vanilla extract
- 1 tbsp baking powder
- 1 large beetroot, precooked and chopped roughly
- 100g/3.5oz chopped dark chocolate
- 200ml sunflower oil

PREPARATION:

1. Use a food processor to break up the beetroot into small pieces
2. Add a little salt, the flour, cocoa powder, baking powder, eggs, vanilla extract, and sugar and mix well
3. Add the oil little by little and combine once more
4. Stir the chocolate in by hand and combine well
5. Preheat the oven to 190C/374F, or gas mark 5
6. Take a cake loaf tin and prepare with baking parchment
7. Pour the mixture into the cake tin and bake for 60 minutes, or until completely cooked
8. Leave to cool in the tin and remove once completely cool
9. Slice to serve

CHERRY CAKE

Time 120 minutes, serves 8-10
Net carbs: 70g/2.5oz, Fiber: 2g/0.07oz, Fat: 32g/1.12oz,
Protein: 9g/0.32oz, Kcal: 585

INGREDIENTS:

- 200g/7oz softened butter
- 200g/7oz caster sugar
- 175g/6oz self-raising flour
- 4 medium eggs
- 0.5 tsp almond extract
- 85g/3oz ground almonds
- 100ml milk
- 0.5 tsp baking powder
- 2 tbsp flaked almonds
- 300g/10.5oz glace cherries

PREPARATION:

1. In a large mixing bowl, coming the sugar and butter until smooth
2. Beat the eggs into the mixture, one at a time
3. Using a spatula, fold the flour, almond extract, baking powder, and ground almonds into the mixture
4. Next, fold in the cherries and the milk, combining well
5. Preheat the oven to 160C/320F, or gas mark 3
6. Take a 20cm cake tin, as deep as you can find, and prepare with baking parchment
7. Pour the mixture into the cake tin and bake in the oven for 60 minutes, or until completely cooked
8. Allow to cool inside the tin before removing

BROWNIES & CUPCAKES

POPPYSEED & LEMON CUPCAKES

Time 65 minutes, serves 12

Net carbs: 66g/2.3oz, Fiber: 1g/0.03oz, Fat: 30g/1.05oz,

Protein: 4g/0.14oz, Kcal: 529

INGREDIENTS:

- 175g/6oz caster sugar
- 225g/8oz self-raising flour
- 1 tbsp toasted poppy seeds
- 3 medium eggs
- Zest of 2 lemons
- 175g/6oz melted butter
- 100g/3.5oz yogurt (natural is best)
- 400g/14oz icing sugar
- 225g/8oz softened butter for the icing
- Juice of 1 lemon for the icing
- Yellow food colouring

PREPARATION:

1. In a medium mixing bowl, combine the sugar, zest, flour and poppy seeds

2. In a small bowl, add the yogurt and eggs and beat until pale and smooth

3. Pour the into the bowl of dry ingredients. Then, add the butter

4. Combine well with a stand mixer or a wooden spoon until smooth

5. Preheat your oven to 180C/356F, or gas mark 4

6. Take a muffin tin with 12 holes and line with cupcake cases

7. Pour between the cases equally

8. Bake for 20 minutes, or until completely cooked

9. Allow to sit for a few minutes before removing the cases onto a cooling rack

10. Meanwhile, take a large mixing bowl and add the softened butter. Stir until very smooth and easy to work with

11. Add the icing sugar and juice little by little, stirring constantly

12. Add a little food colouring and continue to stir

13. Take a piping bag and add the mixture, securing the nozzle onto the front

14. Once the cupcakes have cooled, pipe the buttercream onto the cakes individually, using a circular motion. Complete one circle, stop and then an inner circle, and another until the cake is completely iced.

RASPBERRY & CHOCOLATE BROWNIES

Time 50 minutes, serves 15

Net carbs: 44g/1.55oz, Fiber: 2g/0.07oz, Fat: 22g/0.77oz,

Protein: 5g/0.17oz, Kcal: 389

INGREDIENTS:

- 100g/3.5oz milk chocolate, in chunks
- 200g/7oz dark chocolate, in chunks
- 400g/14oz brown sugar
- 250g/8.8oz butter
- 4 medium eggs
- 50g/1.7oz cocoa powder
- 140g/5oz plain flour
- 200g/7oz fresh or frozen raspberries - defrost beforehand if using frozen

PREPARATION:

1. Take a large pan and add the sugar, chocolate (both), and butter and melt over a medium level heat. Stir every so often to ensure a smooth consistency. Once melted, move from the heat and set to one side

2. Once the mixture has cooled a little, one by one add the eggs and combine

3. Add the flour and cocoa using a sieve and stir in carefully

4. Add half the raspberries and combine once more

5. Preheat your oven to 180C/356F, or gas mark 4

6. Take a baking tray, approximately 20x30cm, and prepare with baking parchment

7. Pour onto the tray and smooth over

8. Scatter the remaining raspberries over the top

9. Bake in the oven for 30 minutes

10. Allow to cool and cut into slices

COFFEE ADDICT CUPCAKES

Time 50 minutes, serves 18

Net carbs: 26g/0.92oz, Fiber: 0g/0oz, Fat: 17g/0.59oz,

Protein: 2g/0.42oz, Kcal: 268

INGREDIENTS:

- 140g/5oz softened butter
- 140g/5oz caster sugar
- 140g/5oz self-raising flour
- 3 medium eggs
- 2tbsp espresso combined with 1 tbsp water
- 200g/7oz softened butter for the icing
- 200g/7oz icing sugar
- 50g/1.7oz melted chocolate
- 2tsp espresso combined with 1 tbsp water

PREPARATION:

1. Take a large mixing bowl and combine the butter and softened butter to create a smooth consistency
2. Add one egg and 1 tbsp flour and beat, and repeat the routine with the other two eggs
3. Add the remaining flour and the espresso and combine again
4. Preheat your oven to 170C/338F, or gas mark 3
5. Take 2 x 9 hole muffin tin and prepare with cupcake cases (total of 18 cupcakes)
6. Pour into the cases evenly
7. Bake for 17 minutes, or until completely cooked
8. Remove the tray from the oven and allow to cool
9. Meanwhile, take a medium mixing bowl and add the butter, stirring until smooth
10. Add the icing sugar gradually and continue to stir
11. Stir in the melted chocolate
12. Add the espresso and stir
13. Once the cupcakes have cool, spoon the icing on top or use a piping bag if you prefer a more professional look

SUMPTUOUS CHOCOLATE BROWNIES

Time 50 minutes, serves 16

Net carbs: 17g/0.6oz, Fiber: 0.5g/0.01oz, Fat: 8g/0.28oz,

Protein: 2g/0.07oz, Kcal: 144

INGREDIENTS:

- ◆ 85g/3oz plain flour
- ◆ 185g/6.5oz chilled butter
- ◆ 185g/6.5oz dark chocolate
- ◆ 40g/1.4oz cocoa powder
- ◆ 50g/1.7oz milk chocolate, cut into chunks
- ◆ 50g/1.7oz white chocolate, cut into chunks
- ◆ 275g/9.7oz caster sugar
- ◆ 3 medium eggs

PREPARATION:

1. Cut the butter into cubes and place in a small pan
2. Add the dark chocolate to the pan
3. Heat on a low heat. Stir until everything is melted, smooth, and combined
4. Take the pan from the heat and place to one side
5. Take a medium mixing bowl and sieve the cocoa powder and flour inside
6. In another mixing bowl, break the eggs and combine until creamy and quite thick
7. Once the chocolate and butter mixture has cooled, pour it into the eggs and use a spatula to fold together, using a figure of eight motion to combine, going as slowly as you can and scraping the edges down regularly
8. Sieve the flour and cocoa mixture into ither bowl and fold once more, using the same figure of eight motion. The mixture will turn into almost a fudge
9. Add the chunks of white and milk chocolate and stir in well
10. Preheat your oven to 180C/356F, or gas mark 4
11. Take a 20cm baking tray and prepare with. Pour the batter inside, smoothing over with a knife
12. Bake for 25 minutes. The brownies should be firm and slightly crusty on top
13. Remove the tray from the oven and cool. Once cool, cut up into squares

FUDGE CHOCOLATE CUPCAKES

Time 55 minutes, serves 12
Net carbs: 56g/1.97oz, Fiber: 2g/0.07oz, Fat: 29g/1oz,
Protein: 5g/0.17oz, Kcal: 509

INGREDIENTS:

- 200g/7oz cooking chocolate or plain chocolate
- 200g/7oz butter
- 2 medium beaten eggs
- 200g/7oz brown sugar
- 1tsp vanilla extract
- 250g/8.8oz self-raising flour
- 200g/7oz plain chocolate for the icing
- 100ml/2.5oz cream (double is best)
- 50g/1.7oz icing sugar

PREPARATION:

1. Take a medium pan and add the butter, cooking/plain chocolate and sugar

2. Add 100ml of water and heat the contents of the pan over a low heat, stirring until everything is melted and smooth

3. Remove the pan from the heat. Set aside to coo

4. Take a large mixing bowl and add the eggs and vanilla, stirring everything together

5. Once the chocolate mixture has cooled, add to the egg mixture and combine

6. Preheat your oven to 160C/F, or gas mark 3

7. Take a 12 holed muffin pan and line with cupcake cases

8. Pour the mixture evenly between the cases

9. Bake for 20 minutes

10. Meanwhile, add take a small pan and melt the plain chocolate over a low heat

11. Remove from the heat once melted and add the cream, stirring all the time

12. Using a sieve, add the icing sugar and combine well. The icing should be thick and spreadable

13. Once the cupcakes have cooled, spread the icing mixture on top, or use a piping bag if you prefer

COOKIES

CLASSIC CHOCOLATE CHIP COOKIES

Time 25 minutes, serves 30

Net carbs: 14.7g/0.5oz, Fiber: 0.5g/0.01oz, Fat: 6.3g/0.22oz,

Protein: 1.3g/0.04oz, Kcal: 121

INGREDIENTS:

- 80g/2.8oz brown sugar
- 80g/2.8oz caster sugar
- 150g/5.3oz softened butter
- 1 medium egg
- 2 tsp vanilla extract

- 0.5tsp bicarbonate soda
- 225g/8oz plain flour
- 200g/7oz chocolate chips
- 0.25 tsp salt

PREPARATION:

1. Into a large mixing bowl, add the softened butter, caster sugar and brown sugar. Mix until a creamy consistency is achieved

2. Add the egg into the bowl and mix once more

3. Add the vanilla extract and combine

4. Using a sieve, add the salt, flour, and bicarbonate soda, and combine with a wooden spoon

5. Pour in the chocolate chips and combine once more

6. Preheat your oven to 190C/374F, or gas mark 5

7. Take a regular sized baking sheet and prepare with parchment

8. Using a spoon or an ice cream scoop, place the dough evenly spaced apart on the sheet

9. Bake in the oven for 10 minutes. The cookies will still be a little soft in the centres but will firm up easily as they cool down

10. Leave the cookies on the tray to cool for a couple of minutes before transferring to a cooling rack

CHEWY GINGER COOKIES

Time 30 minutes, serves 20

Net carbs: 20g/0.7oz, Fiber: 1g/0.03oz, Fat: 5g/0.17oz,

Protein: 1g/0.03oz, Kcal: 135

INGREDIENTS:

- 170g/6oz brown sugar
- 120g/4oz softened butter
- 1.5 tbsp dark treacle
- 1 large egg
- 200g/7oz plain flour
- 60g/2oz caster sugar
- 0.5 tsp sea salt
- 0.25 tsp bicarbonate soda
- 0.25 tsp ground cloves
- 0.5 tsp ground cinnamon
- 1.5 tsp ground ginger

PREPARATION:

1. In a large mixing bowl, combine the brown sugar, salt, butter, and the treacle until smooth
2. Add the spices, egg, flour, and bicarbonate soda to the bowl and combine well
3. Place the mixture in the fridge to chill for around one hour
4. Preheat your oven to 200C/392F, or gas mark 4
5. Take two regular baking trays and line with parchment
6. Remove your cookie dough and create rolled balls of an even size - the mixture should make 20 cookies
7. Take a small place and add the caster sugar
8. Roll the cookie balls in the sugar to coat well
9. Place the cookie balls onto the baking sheet
10. Bake for 10 minutes - the cookies might still be soft in the middle but will firm up
11. Cool for 2 minutes and then transfer to a cooling rack

CHOCOLATE CHUNK COOKIES

Time 50 minutes, serves 12

Net carbs: 36g/1.2oz, Fiber: 2g/0.07oz, Fat: 24g/0.84oz,

Protein: 7g/0.24oz, Kcal: 381

INGREDIENTS:

- ◆ 100g/3.5oz milk chocolate, cut into chunks
- ◆ 300g/10.5oz plain chocolate
- ◆ 85g/3oz butter (ensure the butter is at room temperature)
- ◆ 100g/3.5oz brown sugar
- ◆ 100g/3.5oz peanut butter
- ◆ 100g/3.5oz self-raising flour
- ◆ 100g/3.5oz roasted peanuts
- ◆ 1 large egg
- ◆ 0.5 tsp vanilla extract

PREPARATION:

1. Take 200g/7oz of the plain chocolate and cut it into chunks

2. Place the rest of the plain chocolate in a pan and melt over a low heat

3. Remove the pan and add the egg, butter, vanilla essence, sugar, and peanut butter, beating well until everything is combined

4. Add the flour, nuts, and the milk chocolate chunks and stir to combine

5. Preheat your oven to 180C/356F, or gas mark 4

6. Take two large baking sheets and line them with baking parchments

7. Use an ice cream scoop or a large spoon and drop chunks of the cookie dough onto the baking tray. Make sure you leave enough room between the cookies as they will spread as they're cooking

8. Take the plain chocolate chunks and press them into the top of the dough

9. Bake for 10 minutes. The middles may still be slightly soft

10. Leave on the tray for 2 minutes before transferring to a cooling rack

CRUNCHY BUTTERSCOTCH COOKIES

Time 30 minutes, serves 10

Net carbs: 27g/0.95oz, Fiber: 1g/0.03oz, Fat: 8g/0.28oz,

Protein: 2g/0.07oz, Kcal: 188

INGREDIENTS:

- 100g/3.5oz brown sugar
- 100g/3.5oz softened butter
- 175g/6oz self-raising flour
- 25g/0.9oz puffed rice breakfast cereal
- 2 tbsp golden syrup/treacle

PREPARATION:

1. Take a large mixing bowl and combine the sugar, golden syrup/treacle and butter until soft and smooth

2. Using a sieve, add the flour and mix carefully with a wooden spoon

3. Fold the puffed rice breakfast cereal into the mixture

4. Preheat your oven to 160C/320F, or gas mark 3

5. Take a standard sized baking tray and prepare with baking parchment

6. Using an ice cream scoop or your hands, form equally sized balls with the cookie dough and arrange them on the baking sheet, far enough apart to allow a little spreading

7. Bake in the oven for 20 minutes - the centres will still be a little soft

8. Leave to cool for 2 minutes before moving to a cooling rack

OATY CITRUS COOKIES

Time 50 minutes, serves 16

Net carbs: 19g/0.67oz, Fiber: 2g/0.07oz, Fat: 9g/0.3oz,

Protein: 3g/0.10oz, Kcal: 167

INGREDIENTS:

- 100g/3.5oz brown sugar
- 100g/3.5oz room temperature butter
- 50g/1.7oz mashed banana
- 100g/3.5oz wholemeal flour
- 100g/3.5oz rolled oats
- 50g/1.7oz walnuts, chopped roughly
- 25g/0.8oz desiccated coconut
- 75g/2.6oz sultanas
- 1 medium egg
- 1 tsp vanilla extract
- 0.5 tsp orange zest
- 1 tsp baking powder
- 0.25 tsp salt

PREPARATION:

1. Take a medium mixing bowl and combine the sugar and butter to create a smooth consistency
2. Add the banana and combine well
3. Add the vanilla and egg, combining once more
4. Add the zest and combine everything until smooth
5. In a separate mixing bowl, sieve baking powder, salt, and flour and combine
6. Add the coconut, walnuts, oats, and sultanas and combine well
7. Add the bowl of dry ingredients to the wet and stir well
8. Preheat your oven to 180C/356F, or gas mark 4
9. Take a baking tray and line with baking parchment
10. Using an ice cream scoop or a large spoon, add drops of the cookie dough to the baking tray and press down to flatten a little
11. Bake in the oven for 20 minutes
12. Leave to cool on the tray for a few minutes. Transfer to a cooling rack

SPICY CHOCOLATE COOKIES

SPICY CHOCOLATE COOKIES

Time 30 minutes, serves 40
Net carbs: 17g/0.6oz, Fiber: 1g/0.03oz, Fat: 8g/0.28oz,
Protein: 2g/0.07oz, Kcal: 142

INGREDIENTS:

- 100g/3.5oz caster sugar
- 225g/8oz softened butter
- 175g/6oz brown sugar
- 300g/10.5oz plain flour
- 50g/1.7oz cocoa powder
- 100g/3.5oz chopped dark chilli chocolate
- 100g/3.5oz chopped white chocolate
- 100g/3.5oz chopped dark chocolate
- 1 tsp baking powder
- 2 large beaten eggs
- 2 tsp vanilla extract
- 1.5 tsp cayenne pepper

PREPARATION:

1. In a large mixing bowl, combine the brown sugar, white sugar, and the butter until smooth
2. Slowly add the vanilla and eggs and combine once more
3. In a separate mixing bowl, use a sieve to add the cocoa powder, flour, salt, cayenne pepper, and baking powder
4. Add the powder mixture to the butter/sugar mixture and combine
5. Fold the chocolate pieces into the mixture
6. Preheat your oven to 180C/356F, or gas mark 4
7. Take a large baking tray and prepare with baking parchment
8. Using an Ice cream scoop or a spoon, add drop of the cookie dough onto the baking tray, leaving space between for spreading
9. Bake for 12 minutes - the cookies will be slightly soft in the middle
10. Leave to cool for 2 minutes and then move to the cooling rack

CHOCOLATE PUMPKIN SEED COOKIES

Time 30 minutes, serves 10

Net carbs: 32g/1.12oz, Fiber: 3g/0.11oz, Fat: 19g/0.67oz,

Protein: 5g/0.17oz, Kcal: 328

INGREDIENTS:

- 75g/2.6oz brown sugar
- 75g/2.6oz caster sugar
- 120g/4.2oz softened butter
- 130g/4.5oz plain flour
- 50g/1.7oz pumpkin seeds (toasted work well)
- 150g/5.3oz chunks of dark chocolate
- 1 large egg
- 1 tsp vanilla extract
- 3 tbsp cocoa powder
- 0.5 tsp bicarbonate soda

PREPARATION:

1. In a large mixing bowl, combine the white sugar, brown sugar and butter until smooth

2. Add the vanilla extract and the eggs and combine once more

3. Sieve the bicarbonate soda, flour, and cocoa powder into the bowl combining well

4. Stir in the pumpkin seeds, salt, and chocolate

5. Preheat the oven to 180C/356F, or gas mark 4

6. Take two baking trays and line both with baking parchment

7. Using a large spoon, drop 10 cookies onto the baking tray, leaving enough space in-between as the cookies spread during baking

8. Bake for 10 minutes. The middles will be a little soft but will firm as they cool

9. Allow to cool for a few minutes before transferring to a cooling rack

CHEWY RED COOKIES

Time 35 minutes, serves 16

Net carbs: 36g/1.26oz, Fiber: 1g/0.03oz, Fat: 12g/0.42oz,

Protein: 3g/0.10oz, Kcal: 268

INGREDIENTS:

- 200g/7oz brown sugar
- 100g/3.5oz caster sugar
- 175g/6oz softened butter
- 225g/7.9oz plain flour
- 25g/0.8oz cocoa powder
- 150g/5.2oz white chocolate chips
- 1 medium egg
- 2 tsp vanilla extract
- 0.5 tsp bicarbonate soda
- 1 tbsp red food colouring
- 6 tbsp icing sugar
- 2 tbsp soft cheese

PREPARATION:

1. In a large mixing bowl, add the butter, brown sugar and caster sugar, combining until smooth

2. Add the egg and beat until smooth

3. Next, add the food colouring and the vanilla essence until everything is smooth

4. Using a sieve, add the flour, bicarbonate soda, and vanilla essence

5. Fold everything together using a spoon to create a dough

6. Leave the dough to chill in the refrigerator for one hour

7. Preheat your oven to 190C/374F, or gas mark 5

8. Take a large baking tray and prepare with baking parchment

9. Form medium sized balls with the dough and place them on the baking sheet, pressing down to form a cookie shape. Make sure there is enough space between the cookies for spreading

10. Cook in the oven for 15 minutes. The cookies will be firm yet slightly soft in the middle

11. Allow to cool for a minute before moving to a cooling rack

12. Meanwhile, take a medium mixing bowl and combine the icing sugar and soft cheese to create a smooth mixture

13. Add the mixture to a piping bag and draw lines over the top of the cooled cookies

14. Allow the mixture to set

CRUNCHY MANGO COOKIES

Time 30 minutes, serves 14

Net carbs: 17g/0.6oz, Fiber: 1g/0.03oz, Fat: 5g/0.17oz,

Protein: 2g/0.07oz, Kcal: 156

INGREDIENTS:

- 50g/1.7oz caster sugar
- 140g/5oz room temperature butter
- 100g/3.5oz chopped mango (dried works best)
- 175g/6.17oz plain flour
- 1 tbsp maple syrup
- 1 large egg yolk
- 1 tsp vanilla extract

PREPARATION:

1. Using a blender, add the sugar and butter and blitz until smooth
2. Add the mango, vanilla extract, egg yolk, and maple syrup and blitz once more
3. Add the flour and combine once more
4. Add some flour to your worktop and place the dough on top
5. Create a large ball with the dough and put in the fridge for half an hour to chill
6. Flour your work surface once more and roll the dough out with a rolling pin
7. Use a cookie cutter or the top of a glass to cut out your cookies
8. Preheat your oven to 180C/356F, or gas mark 4
9. Add baking parchment to a large baking tray
10. Add the cookies to the tray. Bake for 15 minutes
11. Place on a cooling rack to cool completely

ALMOND COOKIES

Time 35 minutes, serves 34

Net carbs: 5g/0.17oz, Fiber: 0g/0oz, Fat: 2g/0.07oz,

Protein: 1g/0.03oz, Kcal: 47

INGREDIENTS:

- 140g/4.9oz ground almond
- 140g/4.9oz caster sugar
- 2 tbsp plain flour
- 4 large egg whites

PREPARATION:

1. Place the egg whites into a a medium mixing bowl, whisking until peaks form
2. Add the sugar and carry on whisking until a shiny finish appears
3. Using a sieve, add the flour and combine
4. Add the almonds and fold using a spatula
5. Preheat your oven to 160C/320F, or gas mark 3
6. Take 2 regular baking trays and line with baking parchment
7. Spoon 1 tbsp of the cookie mixture onto the trays, leaving enough space for spreading
8. Bake for 20 minutes, until golden and crispy
9. Place on a cooling rack to cool completely

BREADS

TASTY BANANA BREAD

Time 65 minutes, serves 10

Net carbs: 34g/1.2oz, Fiber: 1g/0.03oz, Fat: 13g/0.45oz,

Protein: 3g/0.10oz, Kcal: 268

INGREDIENTS:

- ◆ 140g/4.9oz caster sugar
- ◆ 140g/4.9oz self-raising flour
- ◆ 140g/4.9oz softened butter
- ◆ 50g/1.7oz icing sugar
- ◆ 1 tsp baking powder
- ◆ 2 large, beaten eggs
- ◆ 2 mashed, ripe bananas

PREPARATION:

1. Add the caster sugar and softened butter into a medium bowl, creaming with a spoon until smooth

2. Combine the eggs

3. Add half the flour and combine once more

4. Fold in the baking powder and the rest of the flour

5. Using a spatula, fold in the bananas and make sure everything is mixed together

6. Preheat your oven to 180C/356F, or gas mark 4

7. Prepare a loaf tin with baking parchment

8. Transfer into the tin and smooth over the top

9. Bake in the oven for 50 minutes, or until completely cooked

10. Leave the bread to cool for 10 minutes and place on a cooling rack

11. As the loaf is cooling, take a small mini bowl and combine the icing sugar with 2 or 3 tsp of water, until the icing is pliable but slightly runny

12. Pour the icing in a zig zag pattern over the bread and cut into pieces

BASIC BREAD LOAF

Time 45 minutes, serves 1 large loaf

Net carbs: 38g/1.34oz, Fiber: 2g/0.07oz, Fat: 4g/0.14oz,

Protein: 6g/0.21oz, Kcal: 204

INGREDIENTS:

- ◆ 500g/17.6oz white flour, the strong variety works best with bread
- ◆ 7g/0.24oz fast acting yeast
- ◆ 300ml water
- ◆ 3 tbsp olive oil
- ◆ 2 tsp salt

PREPARATION:

1. Take a large mixing bowl. Add the yeast, flour, and salt, combining slightly

2. Create a small gap in the centre and pour in the oil and the water, mixing with a wooden spoon

3. You can add a little extra water if the dough is hard to work with

4. Add a little flour to your work surface and turn the dough out

5. Knead the dough for 10 minute. It should be smooth and non-sticky

6. Take a large mixing bowl and add a small amount of oil to grease

7. Place into the bowl and cover over with plastic wrap

8. Place the bowl to one side for one hour. It should be twice the size after the hour is up

9. Take a large baking tray and prepare with baking parchment

10. Remove the plastic wrap from the bowl and punch the dough in the middle to release the air, before tipping it out onto your work surface

11. Create a large ball with the dough and transfer it to your baking tray

12. Cover the dough over once more and leave for another hour

13. Preheat your oven to 220C/428F, or gas mark 7

14. Add a little flour on top and cut two criss cross lines over the top

15. Bake in the oven for 30 minutes - when it's done it will make a hollow noise if you tap it underneath

16. Remove the loaf from the tray and place on a cooling rack

INDIAN NAAN BREAD

Time 55 minutes, serves 6

Net carbs: 31g/1.09oz, Fiber: 1g/0.03oz, Fat: 8g/0.28oz,

Protein: 6g/0.21oz, Kcal: 224

INGREDIENTS:

- ♦ 300g/10.5oz strong bread flour
- ♦ 25g/0.88oz melted butter
- ♦ 2 tsp caster sugar
- ♦ 0.25 tsp salt
- ♦ 7g/0.24oz dried yeast
- ♦ 0.5 tsp baking powder
- ♦ 150ml yogurt (natural yogurt works best)
- ♦ 125ml warm water
- ♦ 1 tbsp nigella seeds

PREPARATION:

1. Take a small mixing bowl and add the yeast. Add the water to the bowl and 1 tsp sugar, mixing very slightly

2. Leave the yeast for 15 minutes, until it has a frothy consistency

3. Take a large mixing bowl and add the other 1 tsp sugar, baking powder and salt, combining together

4. Make a gap in the centre and pour in the yogurt, butter, nigella seeds and the yeast, combining well

5. Once the mixture has turned into a dough, bring it together with your hands until it has a very soft consistency

6. Flour your work surface and add the dough, kneading for 10 minutes, until the dough is smooth and doesn't stick to your hands

7. Take a large mixing bowl and add a little oil in the bottom and up the sides, transferring the dough into the bowl and covering over with plastic wrap

8. Leave the dough for 1 hour, or until it is twice the size

9. Take a large baking tray and prepare with baking parchment

10. Once the dough has risen, divide it into six equal balls

11. Cover the dough over with a towel whilst you're not working on them

12. Warm a large frying pan over a medium heat

13. Roll out one of the dough balls until it is around 21 x 13cm

14. Fry the bread on one side and wait for it to puff up in shape. Once it does so, turn over and cook for another 3 or 4 minutes

15. Remove from the heat and brush with a little melted butter

16. Serve warm

CLOUD BREAD

Time 30 minutes, serves 8

Net carbs: 0.2g/0.007oz, Fiber: 0g/0oz, Fat: 5g/0.17oz,

Protein: 3g/0.10oz, Kcal: 59

INGREDIENTS:

- 50g/1.7oz cream cheese
- 0.25 tsp of cream of tartar
- 0.5 tsp nigella seeds
- 4 eggs, with the yolks and whites separated
- A little oil for baking

PREPARATION:

1. Take a medium mixing bowl and add the egg whites. Using a hand or electric whisk, mix together until peaks appear

2. In a large mixing bowl add the yolks, cream of tartar and the cheese and combine together. The mixture will be pale and smooth

3. Using a spatula, fold the egg whites into the mixture

4. Fold the nigella seeds in and add a little salt and pepper

5. Preheat your oven to 150C/300F, or gas mark 2

6. Take two large baking sheets and prepare them with baking parchment

7. Take a ladle and drop the mixture onto the baking sheet

8. Bake in the oven for 20 minutes

9. Leave to cool on the tray for a couple of minutes before placing on a cooling rack

SIMPLE SODA BREAD

Time 45 minutes, serves 10

Net carbs: 36g/1.2oz, Fiber: 5g/0.17oz, Fat: 2g/0.07oz,

Protein: 7g/0.24oz, Kcal: 207

INGREDIENTS:

- ◆ 500g/17.6oz wholemeal flour
- ◆ 400ml milk
- ◆ 1 tsp bicarbonate soda
- ◆ 2 tsp salt
- ◆ 2 tsp honey
- ◆ The juice of 1 lemon

PREPARATION:

1. Take a large mixing bowl and add the flour, bicarbonate and salt, mixing well

2. In a small mixing jug, combine the lemon juice and the milk, tten the honey and combining once more

3. Pour the mixture into the flour and stir with a knife - a slightly wet dough should form

4. Add some flour to your worktop and place the dough on top

5. Shape the dough into a large ball

6. Preheat your oven to 200C/392F, or gas mark 6

7. Take a large baking tray and prepare with baking parchment

8. Place the dough onto the baking tray and cut a criss cross line in the top section with a knife

9. Bake in the oven for 40 minutes

10. Cool on a cooling rack

CLASSIC BREAD ROLLS

Time 55 minutes, serves 8

Net carbs: 48g/1.69oz, Fiber: 8g/0.28oz, Fat: 2g/0.07oz,

Protein: 8g/0.28oz, Kcal: 246

INGREDIENTS:

- 500g/17.6oz strong bread flour
- 7g/0.24oz fast acting yeast
- 325ml warm water
- 2 tsp salt
- 1 tsp caster sugar
- 1 tsp olive oil

PREPARATION:

1. Take a large bowl and add the salt, flour, yeast, and oil
2. Add the water and use a spatula to combine into a messy dough
3. Cover the bowl over with a towel and place to one side for 10 minutes
4. Add a little flour to your work surface and turn the dough out
5. Knead the dough for 10 minutes. It should be smooth and won't stick to your hands
6. Take a large mixing bowl and grease
7. Create a ball with the dough and leave inside the greased bowl. Cover with plastic wrap and leave for an hour.
8. Take a large baking tray and prepare with baking parchment
9. Divide the dough into 8 equally sized buns and add to the baking tray
10. Preheat your oven to 230C/446F, or gas mark 8
11. Bake in the oven for 25 minutes, checking the rolls are cooked by tapping on the bottom - you should hear a hollow sound
12. Allow the rolls to cool on a cooling rack

CRUNCHY GARLIC BREAD

Time 20 minutes, serves 6

Net carbs: 19g/0.67oz, Fiber: 1g/0.03oz, Fat: 11g/0.38oz,

Protein: 3g/0.10oz, Kcal: 192

INGREDIENTS:

- 1 large baguette, part-baked
- 60g/2.1oz softened butter
- 2 crushed garlic cloves

PREPARATION:

1. In a small mixing bowl, combine the garlic and butter to form a soft consistency
2. Place onto a length of plastic wrap and roll up into a long, thin shape
3. Allow to chill in the fridge for 10 minutes
4. Preheat your oven to 200C/F, or gas mark 6
5. Take the part-baked baguette and cut 12 half-depth lines into the baguette, not cutting all the way
6. Cut the garlic butter mixture into 12 pieces and slot one into each of the bread lines
7. Place the baguette into foil and wrap carefully
8. Take a large baking tray and place the bread onto it
9. Bake for 5 minutes
10. Peel the foil back and bake for another 4 minutes, to brown the bread

FRUITY FIG BREAD ROLLS

Time 70 minutes, serves 20

Net carbs: 43g/1.51oz, Fiber: 4g/0.14oz, Fat: 7g/0.24oz,

Protein: 7g/0.24oz, Kcal: 248

INGREDIENTS:

- 400g/14oz wholemeal flour
- 300ml warm water
- 7g/0.24oz fast acting yeast
- 175g/6.2oz wholemeal flour (separate measurement)
- 400g/14oz strong white flour (separate measurement)
- 7g/0.24oz fast acting yeast (separate measurement)
- 2 tsp salt
- 1 tbsp golden syrup/treacle
- 140g/4.9oz melted butter
- 225ml warm water (separate measurement)
- 100g/3.5oz chopped dates
- 200g/7oz chopped figs

PREPARATION:

1. Take a mixing bowl and combine the first 400g/14oz wholemeal flour, 7g/0.24oz yeast and 300ml water until a dough forms

2. Add some flour to your work surface and turn out the dough, kneading for 10 minutes

3. Take a large mixing bowl and grease a little, placing the dough into the bowl, covering over with plastic wrap and place in the refrigerator overnight

4. Take another large mixing bowl and add the flour, yeast, and salt

5. In another bowl, combing the treacle and butter

6. Make a gap in the centre of the flour bowl and pour in the treacle mixture

7. Add the rest of the dry ingredients (except the fruit) and most of the water, combing well

8. Add a little flour to your work surface and turn out the dough

9. Knead for 10 minutes

10. Take a large mixing bowl and grease, placing the dough inside, covering with plastic wrap and placing to one side for an hour. The dough should double in size

11. Add some flour to your work surface and turn out the dough, adding the dough that you left overnight to combine. Press down into a flat rectangle

12. Sprinkle the fruit over the top and roll up the dough into a long sausage shape, kneading it down once more to distribute the fruit

13. Cut the dough into 20 pieces of even shape and create rolls

14. Cover over for an hour to double in size once more

15. Preheat your oven to 220C/428F, or gas mark 7

16. Bake the rolls for 20 minutes

17. Allow to cool on a cooling rack

BRAZILIAN CHEESY BREAD

Time 50 minutes, serves 24

Net carbs: 11g/0.38oz, Fiber: 0.1g/0.003oz, Fat: 6g/0.21oz,

Protein: 2g/0.07oz, Kcal: 111

INGREDIENTS:

- 300g/10.5oz tapioca flour
- 100g/3.5oz grated parmesan cheese
- 250g/8.8oz room temperature butter
- 1tsp salt
- 250ml milk
- 2 large eggs

PREPARATION:

1. Take a medium sized pan and add the butter, salt, and milk. Allow the pan to reach boiling point and then remove and place to one side

2. Add the flour and stir well, before setting the pan aside to cool a little

3. Pour the dough into a bowl and combine with an electric stand mixer to cool more

4. Add the eggs one at a time and beat

5. Add the cheese and beat again

6. Take a large baking try and prepare with baking parchment

7. Preheat your oven to 220C/428F, or gas mark 7

8. Create small balls out of the dough and place on the tray, leaving enough room between for spreading

9. Bake for half an hour

10. Allow to cool a little and enjoy whilst still warm

HEALTHY FLATBREAD

Time 75 minutes, serves 12

Net carbs: 34g/oz, Fiber: 3g/oz, Fat: 3g/oz,

Protein: 7g/oz, Kcal: 189

INGREDIENTS:

- ◆ 400g/oz strong bread flour
- ◆ 7g/oz dried yeast
- ◆ 2 tbsp warm water, and another 500ml warm water
- ◆ 200g/oz wholemeal bread flour
- ◆ 1 tsp caster sugar
- ◆ 2 tbsp sesame seeds
- ◆ 1 tbs nigella seeds
- ◆ 1 tsp salt

PREPARATION:

1. Take a small mixing bowl and add the yeast, sugar, and 2 tbsp warm water, setting aside for a few minutes

2. In a large mixing bowl, add the two types of flour and salt, combining together

3. Make a hole in the middle of the mixture and add 500ml warm water

4. Using a wooden spoon, mixing into a dough

5. Add a little flour to your work surface and turn out the dough

6. Knead for 10 minutes until the dough is smooth and doesn't stick to your fingers

7. Grease a large mixing bowl slightly and place the dough inside, covering over with a towel placing to one side for 60 minutes. The dough should be twice the size afterwards

8. Add some flour to your work surface, punch the dough in the bowl to release the air and turn out onto the work surface

9. Sprinkle the nigella seeds onto the dough and knead until they're all incorporated evenly

10. Divide the dough into 12 pieces, all even

11. Roll out each piece with a rolling pin, as thin as you can get it

12. Take a large frying pan and add a little oil - make sure the pan is hot before you begin cooking

13. Cook the bread for 2 minutes on each side - bubbles will appear as they cook

14. Eat whilst still slightly warm or wrap in foil and enjoy later

PIES

LEMON MERINGUE PIE

Time 105 minutes, serves 8

Net carbs: 64g/2.25oz, Fiber: 1g/0.03oz, Fat: 24g/0.84oz,

Protein: 7g/0.24oz, Kcal: 480

INGREDIENTS:

- ◆ 175g/6oz plain flour
- ◆ 1 tbsp icing sugar
- ◆ 1 egg yolk
- ◆ 100g/3.5oz cold, cubed butter
- ◆ 100g/3.5oz caster sugar
- ◆ 2 tbsp cornflour
- ◆ 85g/2.9oz room temperature butter, cubed
- ◆ Zest of 2 large lemons
- ◆ Juice of 3 lemons
- ◆ Juice of 1 orange
- ◆ 1 medium egg (whole)
- ◆ 3 egg yolks (for the filling)
- ◆ 4 room temperature egg whites
- ◆ 2 tsp cornflour (extra measurement)
- ◆ 200g/7oz caster sugar (extra measurement)

PREPARATION:

1. First, create the pastry bottom. Add the plain flour, cubed cold butter, 1 tbsp icing sugar and the egg yolk into your food processor. Add 1 tbsp cold water and pulse to make a pastry

2. Add a little flour onto your work surface and turn out the pastry, creating a smooth mixture and rolling out with a rolling pain

3. Take a springform flan tin, measuring 23 x 2.5cm and line the bottom with the pastry, cutting off the edges

4. Stab the pastry bottom with a fork to create small air hole and layer foil over the top

5. Place in the refrigerator for 60 minutes to chill

6. Preheat your oven to 200C/392F, or gas mark 6

7. Take a large baking sheet and add baking parchment

8. Take the pastry out of the fridge and fill with dry baking beans, cooking the pastry blind for 15 minutes

9. Remove the pastry from the oven and set aside

10. Meanwhile, take a medium sized pan and add the 2 tbsp cornflour 100g/3.5oz caster sugar and the lemon zest, combining over a low heat

11. Once combined, add the lemon juice and stir, next add the orange juice and stir once more. Keep staring until a thick mixture appears

12. Add the rest of the butter and allow it to melt, stirring continuously

13. In a small bowl, beat together the 3 egg yolks and the whole egg, before add to the pan and stirring once more

14. The mixture will boil and thicken, so be sure to keep stirring to avoid burning

15. Remove from the heat and place to one side

16. Take a large mixing bowl and add the 4 egg whites. Using a whisk, combine to create peaks

17. Spoon the 100g/3.5oz caster sugar at a time and stir gently

18. Add the cornflour and the remaining sugar and combine until thick

19. Pour into the case and add the meringue on top, starting at the edges, spreading around gently

20. Return to the seven for another 20 minutes. The meringue should be brown and crispy

21. Allow to cool for half an hour

PUMPKIN PIE

Time 90 minutes, serves 8

Net carbs: 45g/1.58oz, Fiber: 2g/0.07oz, Fat: 18g/0.63oz,

Protein: 5g/0.17oz, Kcal: 357

INGREDIENTS:

- ◆ 750g/26.4oz peeled and deseeded pumpkin, cubed
- ◆ 350g/12.3oz shortcrust pastry (sweet)
- ◆ 140g/4.9oz caster sugar
- ◆ 25g/0.8oz melted butter
- ◆ 1 tbsp icing sugar
- ◆ 0.5 tsp salt
- ◆ 1 tsp cinnamon
- ◆ 0.5 tsp grated nutmeg
- ◆ 175ml milk
- ◆ 2 beaten eggs

PREPARATION:

1. Take a large saucepan and add the pumpkin cubes, add a little water (to cover the top) and allow to reach boiling point. Once this occurs, cover the pan over and simmer for around 15-20 minutes to tenderise

2. Drain the water and place the pumpkin to one side to cool

3. Take your sweet shortcrust pastry and roll it out flat

4. Take a springform tart tin, around 22cm in size

5. Line with the pastry and place in the fridge to chill for 15 minutes

6. Remove the tin from the fridge and add baking parchment over the top and baking beans

7. Preheat your oven to 180C/356F, or gas mark 4

8. Bake blind for 15 minutes

9. Remove the beans and parchment and return to the oven for another 20 minutes, browning up the base

10. Remove and place to one side to cool

11. Turn your oven up to 220C/428F, or gas mark 7

12. Take a large mixing bowl and add the nutmeg, sugar, salt, and half the cinnamon , combining well

13. Add the butter, milk, and eggs, combining well

14. Add the pumpkin and combine to make a puree mixture

15. Transfer into the case

16. Bake for 10 minutes before turning the oven down to 180C/356F, or gas mark 4

17. Bake for half an hour - the centre should firm up

18. Cool for a few minutes before removing the pie from the tart tin

19. Cool completely on a cooling rack

FAIL-PROOF APPLE PIE

Time 60 minutes, serves 4

Net carbs: 52g/1.8oz, Fiber: 5g/0.17oz, Fat: 31g/1.09oz,

Protein: 8g/0.28oz, Kcal: 527

INGREDIENTS:

- 225g/7.9oz plain flour
- 140g/4.9oz room temperature butter
- 2 tbsp honey
- 1 beaten egg
- 3 cooking apples
- 0.25 tsp mixed spice
- 0.25 tsp cinnamon
- 3 tbsp water, and an extra 2 tbsp water

PREPARATION:

1. Take a large mixing bowl and add the butter and flour
2. Crumble the mixture by hand before gradually adding 3 tbsp of water, bringing the mixture together
3. Wrap the pastry in plastic wrap and place in the refrigerator for 30 minutes
4. Cut the skin and the core from the apples and create small chunks
5. Take a regular sized pie dish and arrange the apples over the bottom
6. Pour the honey evenly over the apples and sprinkle the mixed spice and cinnamon too
7. Pour 2 tbsp water over the mixture evenly
8. Add a little flour to your work surface and take the pastry from the fridge, rolling it out evenly and ensuring it is large enough to cover the top of the dish
9. Lay the pastry on top of the dish and cut away the edges. If you don't want to throw them away you can layer them over the top in a pattern
10. Use a fork to seal the pie edges and stab the top a few times to let out the steam
11. Brush the egg on top of the pie
12. Preheat your oven to 200C/392F, or gas mark 6
13. Bake in the oven for 30 minutes and cool before serving

CARIBBEAN LIME PIE

Time 40 minutes, serves 8

Net carbs: 54g/1.9oz, Fiber: 0g/0oz, Fat: 46g/1.6oz,

Protein: 7g/0.24oz, Kcal: 661

INGREDIENTS:

- 85g/3oz melted butter
- 225g/7.9oz ginger biscuits
- 405g/14.2oz condensed milk
- 320g/11.2oz coconut cream
- Zest and juice of 6 limes
- 2 tbsp icing sugar
- 300ml double cream

PREPARATION:

1. Use a food processor to blitz the ginger biscuits. They should resemble small crumbs

2. Add the butter and combine

3. Take a tart tin, around 22cm in size and add the crumbs to the bottom, pressing down to make a firm base. Place in the refrigerator for 10 minutes

4. Take a large saucepan and add the zest and juice, condensed milk, 100ml of the cream, coconut cream and combine together

5. Turn the heat to medium, allow to boil and then turn down to a simmer, allowing the mixture to bubble for around 5 minutes

6. Pour into the case

7. Chill in the refrigerator and for 3 hours. The mixture should be completely set

8. In a small mixing bowl, combine the icing sugar with rest of the cream. Layer over the pie, starting in the centre and moving outwards

STICKY BANOFFEE PIE

Time 25 minutes, serves 10

Net carbs: 43g/1.5oz, Fiber: 1g/0.03oz, Fat: 36g/1.26oz,

Protein: 5g/0.17oz, Kcal: 518

INGREDIENTS:

- 225g/7.9oz biscuits, digestive work well here
- 400g/14oz dulce de leche
- 1 tbsp icing sugar
- 150g/5.2oz melted butter
- 300ml cream, double works best
- 3 small, sliced bananas

PREPARATION:

1. Bash the biscuits with a rolling pin to make crumbs, or place them in a food processor and blitz if you prefer

2. Pour the biscuits into a medium mixing bowl and add the melted butter, stirring to combine

3. Take a tart tin, around 23cm in size, and add the biscuits to the bottom, pressing down to create a firm layer

4. Place the tin in the refrigerator for around 1 hour to set

5. Pour the dulce de leche into a medium mixing bowl and stir to loosen up

6. Spread the mixture over the tin base using a knife

7. Arrange the banana over the top and place back in the refrigerator

8. In a medium mixing bowl, combine the cream and the icing sugar to create a thick consistency

9. Spread the mixture over the top of the pie, starting in the middle and working your way outwards

MUD PIE

Time 90 minutes, serves 10

Net carbs: 49g/1.7oz, Fiber: 4g/0.14oz, Fat: 50g/1.7oz,

Protein: 7g/0.24oz, Kcal: 680

INGREDIENTS:

- 100g/3.5oz melted butter
- 308g/10.8oz chocolate biscuits
- 100g/3.5oz room temperature butter
- 140g/4.9oz chopped dark chocolate
- 140g/4.9oz brown sugar
- 25g/0.8oz plain flour
- 2 large eggs
- 50g/1.7oz dark chocolate (separate measurement)
- 500g/17.6oz vanilla custard (pre-made is easier)
- 3 sheets of gelatine
- 0.5 tsp vanilla extract
- 300ml double cream

PREPARATION:

1. Bash the biscuits with a rolling pin or blitz them in the food processor to create crumbs

2. Take a medium bowl and add the biscuits. Pour the melted butter over the top and stir

3. Take a pie dish, around 24cm in size, and press the biscuits into the bottom, to create a firm base

4. Preheat your oven to 180C/356F, or gas mark 4

5. Bake in the oven for 10 minutes to create a firmer layer

6. Take out of the oven and place to one side

7. Take a small pan and melt the room temperature butter and 140g/4.9oz dark chocolate, combining well

8. Remove from the heat

9. In a medium bowl, combine the eggs with a whisk. They should be pale and then add the sugar and combining again

10. Using a spatula, fold the chocolate and butter mixture

11. Use a sieve to add the flour and fold once more

12. Transfer the mixture to the pie dish and smooth out

13. Bake in the oven for 20 minutes - a crust should have formed on top

14. Remove from the oven and place to one side

15. Take a small pan and add the custard, vanilla extract and remaining chocolate, stirring over a medium heat. Place to one side once combined

16. Soak the gelatine sheets with a little water in a large dish, until soft. Shake off the water and place in the pan, stirring until melted

17. Allow the mixture to cool a little before pouring on the pie tin

18. Transfer to the refrigerator for 2 hours, until everything is completely set

SUMPTUOUS COOKIE PIE

Time 90 minutes, serves 24

Net carbs: 70g/2.4oz, Fiber: 4g/0.14oz, Fat: 32g/1.1oz,

Protein: 7g/0.24oz, Kcal: 610

INGREDIENTS:

- ♦ 450g/15.8oz brown sugar
- ♦ 3 tbsp vanilla paste
- ♦ 250g/8.8oz softened butter
- ♦ 450g/15.8oz self-raising flour
- ♦ 3 tbsp milk
- ♦ 150g/5.3oz chocolate chips
- ♦ 450g/15.8oz chopped dark chocolate
- ♦ 330g/11.6oz softened butter (separate measurement)
- ♦ 6 medium eggs
- ♦ 225g/7.9oz plain flour
- ♦ 500g/17.6oz caster sugar

PREPARATION:

1. Take a large mixing bowl and add the brown sugar and 250g/8.8oz butter. Use a stand mixer to beat together until smooth

2. Add the vanilla and combine once more

3. Sieve in the self-raising flour and combine slowly

4. Add the chocolate chips and stir into the dough until everything is mixed together

5. Place the dough in plastic wrap and leave in the refrigerator

6. Take a medium saucepan and melt the 330g/11.6oz softened butter with the dark chocolate, stirring to combine

7. Remove from the heat and cool

8. Take a pie tin, around 30x40cm and line it with the chilled cookie dough, allowing the dough to come up the sides a little

9. Preheat the oven to 180C/356F, or gas mark 4

10. Bake for 15 minutes and then place to one side

11. Meanwhile, take a medium mixing bowl and mix together the eggs and the sugar

12. Mix this mixture into the melted chocolate and combine well

13. Fold in the plain flour and mix together well

14. Pour this mixture over the top of the baked cookie base and smooth out

15. Return to the oven for an extra 30 minutes

16. Remove from the oven and allow to cool significantly before eating!

PECAN & CHOCOLATE PIE

Time 75 minutes, serves 8

Net carbs: 75g/2.64oz, Fiber:4g/0.14oz, Fat: 63g/2.2oz,

Protein: 13g/0.45oz, Kcal: 898

INGREDIENTS:

- ◆ 185g/6.5oz dark chocolate
- ◆ 50g/1.7oz room temperature butter
- ◆ 375g/13.2oz shortcrust pastry (pre-bought)
- ◆ 200ml maple syrup
- ◆ 4 beaten eggs
- ◆ 200g/7oz pecan nuts

PREPARATION:

1. Take the shortcrust pasty and roll out

2. Take a springform tart tin, around 20cm in size and lay the pastry inside, cutting around the top edges

3. Place baking parchment and baking beans inside the tin

4. Preheat your oven to 180C/356F, or gas mark 4

5. Bake for 25 minutes. Remove the beans and parchment and cook for another 10 minutes

6. Meanwhile, take a medium pan and melt the butter and chocolate over a low heat, stirring continuously. Remove from the heat once combined

7. Take a large mixing bowl and combine the eggs and maple syrup

8. Add the chocolate mixture and stir well, adding the nuts as you go along

9. Pour the mixture into the tart tin and add a few remaining nuts on top for decoration

10. Cook for half an hour

11. Make sure everything is completely cool before you serve

CLASSIC CHERRY PIE

Time 60 minutes, serves 10

Net carbs: 66g/2.3oz, Fiber: 3g/0.10oz, Fat: 25g/0.88oz,

Protein: 8g/0.28oz, Kcal: 523

INGREDIENTS:

- ◆ 400g/14oz plain flour
- ◆ 225g/7.9oz chilled butter
- ◆ 50g/1.7oz ground almonds
- ◆ 2tbsp extra ground almonds
- ◆ 2 egg yolks
- ◆ 75g/2.6oz caster sugar
- ◆ 150g/5.3oz cherry flavoured jam
- ◆ 800g/28oz fresh or frozen cherries (defrost first), with stones removed
- ◆ 50g/1.7oz caster sugar (separate measurement)
- ◆ 1 egg white
- ◆ 2.5 tbsp cornflour
- ◆ 2 tbsp water

PREPARATION:

1. Take a food processor and add the 50g/1.7oz almonds, butter, 75g/2.6oz sugar and flour. Pulse until crumbs appear

2. Add the water and egg yolks and mix once more

3. Add flour to your work surface and turn out the pastry, creating a smooth ball

4. Cut the pastry into two balls and wrap both in separate pieces of plastic wrap. Chill in the refrigerator for 30 minutes

5. Take a large mixing bowl and combine the cherries, remaining sugar, jam, and cornflour

6. Preheat your oven to 200C/392F, or gas mark 6

7. Roll out the two balls of pastry into two flat pieces

8. Take a pie dish, around 25cm in size

9. Lay one piece of pastry over the pie dish base and allow to reach up the sides, cutting off the excess

10. Add the extra almonds along the bottom layer and then spoon the cherry mixture inside, smoothing out evenly

11. Cover the top with the other layer of pastry and stab holes in the top to allow the steam to come out

12. You can decorate the top of the pie with any cut off pastry you have left

13. Seal the edges of the pie with a fork and sprinkle the icing sugar over the top

14. Bake in the oven for 1 hour, and cool another 1 hour before cutting

FUDGE BROWNIE PIE

Time 90 minutes, serves 8

Net carbs: 71g/oz, Fiber: 2g/oz, Fat: 38g/oz,

Protein: 7g/oz, Kcal: 639

INGREDIENTS:

- 17g/oz plain flour
- 85g/oz chilled, cubed butter
- 3 medium eggs
- 2 tbsp icing sugar
- 1 tsp cinnamon
- 300g/oz brown sugar
- 175g/oz melted butter
- 1 tsp vanilla extract
- 50g/oz plain flour
- 50g/oz cocoa powder
- 50g/oz chopped macadamia nuts
- 50g/oz chopped dark chocolate

PREPARATION:

1. Add the plain flour, chopped butter, brown sugar and cinnamon into your food processor and pulse to create crumbs

2. Add a little water to loosen the mixture up and bring together

3. Wrap the mixture in a sheet of plastic wrap. Chill in the refrigerator for 20 minutes

4. Remove from the wrap and roll out

5. Take a springform tart tin, around 23cm in size and line the bottom with the pastry, cutting off the edges towards the top

6. Add baking parchment inside and add baking beans

7. Preheat the oven to 180C/F, or gas mark 4

8. Place in the oven for 15 minutes. Remove the beans and paper. Return to the seven for 5 minutes

9. In a large mixing bowl combine the sugar and eggs to create a smooth mixture and add the vanilla and butter

10. Using a spatula, fold in the cocoa powder and plain flour

11. Sprinkle the nuts over the top of the pastry case and then pour the chocolate mixture over the top and smooth down

12. Place back in the oven for 30 minutes. The top section should still move a little

13. Allow to cool before serving

CRUMBLES AND MORE

AUTHENTIC NEW YORK CHEESECAKE

Time 70 minutes, serves 12

Net carbs: 37g/1.3oz, Fiber: 1g/0.03oz, Fat: 41g/1.4oz,

Protein: 11g/0.38oz, Kcal: 549

INGREDIENTS:

- 140g/4.9oz digestive style biscuits, crushed into crumbs
- 1 tbsp caster sugar for the bottom crust
- 250g/8.8oz caster sugar for the filling
- 900g/31oz soft cheese
- 3 tbsp plain flour
- Zest of 1 lemon
- 1.5 tsp vanilla extract
- 1.5 tsp lemon juice
- 284ml sour cream for the filling
- 3 medium eggs
- 142ml sour cream from the topping
- 2 tsp lemon juice for the topping

PREPARATION:

1. Take a springform cake tin and prepare with baking parchment
2. Take a medium pan and add the butter, heating until melted. Then, add the crumbs, the 1 tbsp sugar, and mix everything together
3. Once cooled slightly, add the mixture into the cake tin and press down to create a firm base
4. Using a stand mixer, combine the soft cheese with the 250g/8.8oz sugar, and flour
5. Add the lemon zest, juice and vanilla and combine once more
6. Add the eggs and combine again
7. Using a wooden spoon, add the 284ml sour cream until the mixture is smooth and light
8. Add the filling to the cake tin and smooth over
9. Preheat your oven to 200C/392F, or gas mark 6
10. Place back in the oven and bake for 10 minutes, before reducing the heat down to 100C/212F, or gas mark 1/4, baking for another 45 minutes
11. Remove from the oven and set aside
12. In a mixing bowl, combine the sugar, lemon juice and remaining sour cream
13. Cover the cheesecake and refrigerate overnight

WARMING RHUBARB CRUMBLE

Time 60 minutes, serves 4

Net carbs: 68g/2.3oz, Fiber: 3g/0.1oz, Fat: 18g/0.63oz,

Protein: 4g/0.14oz, Kcal: 440

INGREDIENTS:

- 100g/3.5oz caster sugar
- 500g/17.6oz chopped rhubarb
- 140g/4.9oz self-raising flour
- 85g/3oz chilled butter
- 50g/1.7oz brown sugar

PREPARATION:

1. Take a large saucepan and add the rhubarb, sugar and enough water to cover over the top
2. Simmer for around 15 minutes, until the rhubarb is soft
3. Add the butter and flour into a large bowl and use your fingers to make a crumble
4. Add the brown sugar and combine well
5. Preheat your oven to 200C/392F, or gas mark 6
6. Take a medium baking dish and add the cooled rhubarb along the bottom
7. Pour the crumble on top and cover completely
8. Bake in the oven for 30 minutes and allow to cool before serving

APPLE CRUMBLE BREAD

Time 90 minutes, serves 10

Net carbs: 45g/1.5oz, Fiber: 2g/0.07oz, Fat: 17g/0.59oz,

Protein: 5g/0.17oz, Kcal: 350

INGREDIENTS:

- 250g/8.8oz self-raising flour
- 140g/4.9oz brown sugar
- 140g/4.9oz chilled, cubed butter
- 2 tsp mixed spice
- 100g/3.5oz raisins
- 5 tbsp milk
- 3 large, beaten eggs
- 2 peeled, cored, and chopped cooking apples
- 1 tbsp plain flour
- 25g/0.8oz room temperature butter
- 25g/0.8oz brown sugar (separate measurement)
- 1 tbsp chopped hazelnuts

PREPARATION:

1. Take a loaf tin, around 2 litres in size, and prepare with baking parchment
2. Add the spices and self-raising flour into a food processor and use to combine
3. Add the sugar and combine once more
4. In a large mixing bowl, add the apples, milk, and raisins and combine once more
5. Add the flour mixture and combine again. Transfer the mixture into the tin
6. Take another large mixing bowl and add the plain flour, 25g/0.8oz butter and 25g/0.8oz sugar and use your fingers to rub together into a crumble
7. Add the crumble on top of the tin
8. Preheat your oven to 160C/320F, or gas mark 3
9. Bake in the oven for 55 minutes
10. Cool for a few minutes. Turn the loaf out of the tin and cool on a rack

CLASSIC SCONES

Time 15 minutes, serves 8

Net carbs: 41g/oz, Fiber: 1g/oz, Fat: 10g/oz,

Protein: 6g/oz, Kcal: 268

INGREDIENTS:

- 350g/oz self-raising flour
- 1 tsp baking powder
- 0.25 tsp salt
- 3 tbsp caster sugar
- 85g/oz chilled, cubed butter
- 175ml milk
- 1 tsp vanilla extract
- 1 beaten egg
- 0.25 tsp lemon juice

PREPARATION:

1. Take a large mixing bowl. Add the salt, flour, baking powder, combining together
2. Add the cubed butter and use your fingers to rub the ingredients together into breadcrumbs
3. Take a small saucepan and warm up the milk. Don't allow the milk to get too hot, you need it warm enough to touch only
4. Add the vanilla extract and lemon juice, stir and place to one side
5. Take a baking tray and prepare with baking parchment
6. Preheat the oven to 220C/F, or gas mark 7
7. Add the wet ingredients into the dry. Using a knife, mix everything together
8. Add some flour to your work surface and turn out the mixture
9. Fold the dough a few times until it's easier to work with
10. Use a cookie cutter to create circles around 5cm in depth
11. Brush a little egg on the top of the scones
12. Arrange the scones on the tray and bake for 10 minutes
13. Allow to cool slightly before removing onto a cooling rack

BAKED ALASKA

Time 35 minutes, serves 8

Net carbs: 102g/3.59oz, Fiber: 10g/0.35oz, Fat: 21g/0.74oz,

Protein: 9g/0.31oz, Kcal: 609

INGREDIENTS:

- 200g/7oz black cherry jam
- 400g/14oz vanilla flavoured ice cream
- 200g/7oz toffee or caramel flavoured ice cream
- 200g/7oz caster sugar
- 5 egg whites
- 400g/14oz pre-bought fruit cake

PREPARATION:

1. Take a large and deep pudding bowl, around 900ml depth, and line with plastic wrap
2. Take the caramel ice cream and place in the bottom of the bowl, pushing down to the very bottom
3. Add the jam and spread over the top in an even layer
4. Add the vanilla ice cream in another layer
5. Push everything down gently and cover over with more plastic wrap
6. Place in the freezer for 2 hours
7. Preheat the oven to 200C/392F, or gas mark 6
8. Take a medium bowl and combine the egg whites until peaks form, before adding the sugar and combining again
9. Take a baking sheet and cut a piece of baking parchment the same size as the top of the bowl. Arrange pieces of the fruit cake to fit the shape, making sure there are no spaces in-between
10. Remove the bowl from the freezer and take the plastic wrap off
11. Turn the ice cream onto the top of the pre-arranged cake and press down the bowl firmly before removing it
12. Spread the meringue mixture on top evenly
13. Bake for 5 minutes, to crisp up the top
14. Serve whilst hot

CLASSIC FLAPJACKS

Time 30 minutes, serves 12

Net carbs: 27g/0.95oz, Fiber: 2g/0.07oz, Fat: 10g/0.35oz,

Protein: 2g/0.07oz, Kcal: 212

INGREDIENTS:

♦ 125g/4.4oz room temperature butter

♦ 250g/8.8oz porridge oats

♦ 125g/4.4oz brown sugar

♦ 3 tbsp golden syrup/treacle

PREPARATION:

1. Take your food processor and mix together the butter, oats, syrup/treacle and sugar until everything is combined well

2. Take a baking tin, around 20x20cm, and line with baking parchment

3. Preheat your oven to 200C/392F, or gas mark 6

4. Add the mixture to the baking tin and press down until firm and flat

5. Bake in the oven for 15 minutes

6. Allow to cool. Remove from the tin and cut into squares

EASY MERINGUE NESTS

Time 75 minutes, serves 16

Net carbs: 31g/1.09oz, Fiber: 0g/0oz, Fat: 9.6g/0.33oz,

Protein: 2.1g/0.07oz, Kcal: 210

INGREDIENTS:

- ◆ 115g/4oz caster sugar
- ◆ 115g/4oz icing sugar
- ◆ 4 large egg whites

PREPARATION:

1. Take two large baking sheets and prepare with baking parchments
2. Take a large mixing bowl and add the egg whites. Beat with an electric whisk until they're fluffy and form peaks
3. Turn your mixer up and slowly add the caster sugar gradually, continuing to beat between. The meringue is ready when it's shiny and quite thick in consistency
4. Using a sieve add a third of the icing sugar and use a spatula to fold it in carefully
5. Add the rest of the icing sugar in the same way
6. Preheat your oven to 110C/230F, or gas mark 1/4
7. Using a large spoon, place the mixture on the tray in any shape you like
8. Bake in the oven for 1.5 hours
9. Allow to cool on a wire rack

APPLE & DATE TREATS

Time 55 minutes, serves 8

Net carbs: 68g/2.3oz, Fiber: 4g/oz, Fat: 24g/0.14oz,

Protein: 5g/0.17oz, Kcal: 513

INGREDIENTS:

- ◆ 140g/4.9oz peeled, cored, and cubed cooking apples
- ◆ 225g/7.9oz room temperature butter
- ◆ 280g/9.8oz brown sugar
- ◆ 2 tbsp water
- ◆ 175g/6oz plain flour
- ◆ 140g/4.9oz chopped dates
- ◆ 100g/3.5oz porridge oats
- ◆ 1 tsp bicarbonate soda

PREPARATION:

1. Take a large saucepan and add the apples and water, covering over and bringing to the boil. Allow to simmer on a lower heat for 5 minutes

2. Add 50g/1.7oz of the sugar and the dates and combine well, cooking for another 5 minutes

3. Remove from the heat and use a fork or a wooden spoon to mash the apples and dates down

4. In a small saucepan, melt the butter over a low heat and set aside

5. Take a large mixing bowl and combine the rest of the sugar, the flour, bicarbonate soda, and the oats. Add the butter and combine everything once more

6. Preheat your oven to 190C/374F, or gas mark 5

7. Take a baking tin, around 18cm in size, and prepare with parchment

8. Take half of the oat mixture down into the bottom of the tin, pressing down with a spoon

9. Spread the apple mixture over the top and press the rest of the oat mixture on top, smoothing to give an even layer

10. Bake in the oven for 30 minutes

11. Allow to cool before cutting into square pieces

FRUIT & CARAMEL BLONDIES

Time 60 minutes, serves 12

Net carbs: 46g/1.6oz, Fiber: 2g/0.07oz, Fat: 23g/0.8oz,

Protein: 5g/0.17oz, Kcal: 413

INGREDIENTS:

- ◆ 275g/9.7oz brown sugar
- ◆ 250g/8.8oz chilled, cubed butter
- ◆ 25g/0.8oz muscovado sugar
- ◆ 3 medium eggs
- ◆ 1 tsp vanilla extract
- ◆ 200g/7oz plain flour

- ◆ 1 tsp baking powder
- ◆ 1 tsp salt
- ◆ 3 tbsp caramel
- ◆ 100g/3.5oz chopped, dried pears
- ◆ 100g/3.5oz chopped dark chocolate

PREPARATION:

1. In a small saucepan, melt the butter over a medium heat and place to one side

2. Take a large mixing bowl and add the eggs, whisking until pale and frothy

3. Add the two sugars and combine once more

4. Add the vanilla, salt and the melted butter and combine again

5. Using a spatula, fold the baking powder, flour, pears, and the chocolate (leaving a small amount aside for decoration)

6. Preheat your oven to 180C/356F, or gas mark 4

7. Take a square tin, around 20x20cm in size, and line with baking parchment

8. Transfer the mixture into the tin and sprinkle the rest of the chocolate on top, dropping the caramel over the top too

9. Bake for 40 minutes

10. Allow to cool in the tin before cutting into squares

COFFEE MILLIONAIRE'S SHORTBREAD

Time 80 minutes, serves 18

Net carbs: 52g/1.83oz, Fiber: 3g/0.10oz, Fat: 27g/0.95oz,

Protein: 7g/0.24oz, Kcal: 482

INGREDIENTS:

- 250g/8.8oz plain flour
- 75g/2.6oz caster sugar
- 200g/7oz chilled, cubed butter
- 4 tbsp espresso powder
- 100g/3.5oz brown sugar
- 794g/28oz condensed milk
- 50g/1.7oz room temperature butter
- 300g/10.5oz chopped dark chocolate
- 30g/1oz chopped white chocolate
- 1 tsp espresso powder (separate measurement)

PREPARATION:

1. In a large mixing bowl, combine the flour, caster sugar and chilled butter until completely combined - use your hands to bring it together into a workable dough

2. Add some flour to your work surface and turn the dough out, forming a ball

3. Take a baking tin, around 20x30cm and prepare with baking parchment

4. Press the dough down into the bottom of the baking tin, in an even layer

5. Preheat your oven to 180C/356F, or gas mark 4

6. Bake in the oven for 25 minutes and place to one side

7. Meanwhile, take a small mixing bowl and add the 4 tbsp espresso powder with 1 tbsp of hot water and mix

8. Take a heavy pan and add the brown sugar, espresso mixture and the condensed milk, allowing it to simmer until all the sugar has dissolved. Turn the heat up at that point and allow to boil for 3 minutes, stirring continuously. The mixture will be darker in colour and noticeably thicker

9. Remove from the heat and allow to cool for 20 minutes

10. Pour the caramel over the baking tin base and place in the refrigerator for 2 hours

11. In a medium pan, melt the room temperature butter and both chocolate types over a low heat, mixing continuously, before adding the remaining espresso powder

12. Pour the chocolate over the caramel and place back in the refrigerator for another 2 hours

13. Once set, cut into squares.

COFFEE MILLIONAIRE'S SHORTBREAD

Printed in Great Britain
by Amazon